The Art of the Creel

Written by Hugh Chatham and Dan McClain

Photography by Gretchen Duykers

Published by Blue Heron Publications, Ennis, Montana

Designed by Media Works, Bozeman, Montana
Printed in China, Palace Press International
5 4 3 2 1

Published by Blue Heron Publications
Box 1309
Ennis, Montana 59720

ISBN Number 0-9659172-7-4
Library of Congress 97-074370

This book is gratefully dedicated to

Daryll Whitehead

Contents

Foreword

The genesis of this book is the work of Daryll Whitehead. His collection of fishing creels was carefully assembled over a long period of time and included a wide variety of most of the types and makers of creels. In 1996 the publishers of this book acquired Daryll's collection and began working on *The Art of the Creel*. Daryll's referrals led to other collectors who were kind enough to allow their collections to be photographed. As this project progressed, other collections were located and photographed and the scope of the book grew way beyond original expectations; however, without Daryll Whitehead's collection, knowledge, and love of creels, there would be no *The Art of the Creel*.

The author-publishers of this book have worked very hard to provide a comprehensive photographic overview of the subject of fishing creels. We have done our best to include as much accurate and interesting information about the subject as we could find. One purpose that this book can serve, is to provide a base for discussion and information about creels, and we welcome any questions or information about fishing creels. Please contact:

Blue Heron Publications
Box 1309
Ennis, Montana 59729

(406) 682-7171
Toll free: (888) BL HERON
Fax: (406) 682-5086
E-mail: BHERONPUB@AOL.com

Introduction

The creel, the basket to hold fresh fish, has become the icon of the modern fly fishing industry. Creels appear as part of the logos of smart shops, advertising agencies use them for props, decorators put flower pots in them to decorate homes, window trimmers utilize them in department store windows and the cover paintings on old hunting and fishing magazines show creels in use. But one hardly ever sees them on a stream, in the use for which they were intended.

The purpose of the creel was to hold the fisherman's catch, maybe his lunch, a garment such as a rain coat, a bait container or a fly wallet and leaders. Just as a sapling could and did serve as a substitute for a fishing rod, a gunny sack could fill in for the creel and a jacket pocket as a holder for lunch and other items that today would be carried in a vest. As the angler moved up and down the stream, there was need for storage that was portable and handy. What better than a basket? Air could circulate for cooling and a closure of some sort would keep the flopping fish from escaping. And, baskets were readily available.

What is it that makes these containers "Folk Art" rather than just fish holders? There is a relationship between producing a product and art. Art comes from the skill involved in producing the work. It is the matter of individual expression - the added dimension of work well done that raises the ordinary creel to the collectible status.

There were many commercial basket makers. It has been said that every town had one because of the demand for containers. But it was not only the basket weavers who made creels. Fine handcrafters created beautiful wooden boxes in the classic shape of the creel. Others used leather to make the well-known form. Some of these makers went beyond the everyday and their work was worthy of being called "art."

Just as our golf and country clubs fill a social need, so did the hunting and fishing clubs of yesteryear. Those who could afford it took to their camps in the Adirondacks and their fishing cabins on the northern lakes. They fished for companionship. They fished for solitude. They fished to refresh their souls.

Today, with the advent of "catch and release," the angler fishes for all of the above reasons, but he, or she, does not fish to necessarily take fish home. Angling has become "fly fishing" and "fly fishing" has become a way of life and a religion for the high stressed citizens of today. And when one can't fish, one reminds oneself of those wonderful days on the stream by collecting the old tools of the trade. But even more, these old tools—the beautiful cane rod that belonged to grandfather, the creel that came home after father's trip to England, the brass Hardy reel that was found in a second-hand store—have all become the symbols of fly fishing.

The old tools of the trade, once utilitarian, have transformed into collectibles and those made by individuals with very special attributes have become folk art. It is because the creel, once so common and utilitarian, has faded from view that its history and beauty should be saved. These symbols of a sport and of an era, while being gathered in a few collections across the country, need to be recorded for posterity. Here we give you the fishing creel as an art form.

1

Early Creels and Basketry

"With all my heart; boy, take the key of my fishing-house, and carry down …
my fish-pannier, pouch, and landing net…"

F ish pannier is as close to a creel as anything ever mentioned by Isaak Walton in the first edition of *The Compleat Angler* published in 1653. Webster's tells us that a pannier is "a large basket … one carried on the shoulders of a person." Although later editions are illustrated with what appear to be leather creels, it was just nine years after the first publication of *The Compleat Angler* that the frontispiece of Robert Venables' *The Experienced Angler* shows a creel in its classic form.

It is interesting to note, however, that Webster traces the word "creel" or "a wickerwork receptacle" to Middle English and dates it from about 1250 A.D. to 1450 A.D. Because we know that *The Experienced Angler* was published in 1665 and used a willow creel as a part of the frontis, we must assume that the creel in its present form was in use before the 17th century, and probably even earlier than the 16th century. Late in the 17th century, however, leather creels became fashionable. While leather creels did not displace the willow basket, their popularity lasted into the late 18th century. To the left, this example of a leather creel came from England and is dated at around 1720.

English leather creel circa 1700 with brass fittings and fishing motif on top. The design on top has a Waltonian style.

By the middle of the 18th century, when fishing tackle was being exported by London shops to the American colonies, leather creels were still in use in England, but their popularity did not last. Basketry soon took over. Leather was not the only exotic material used to create a creel form. Other early illustrations show wood slats joined in the classical shape. Fine walnut wood creels with lovely brass fittings shaped by some unknown but very skilled craftsman certainly fit into the collectable category of fishing creels. A late American entry shown here is made of leather and dates from the early to mid-19th century.

Walnut creel with brass latch and corners from England circa 1800.

American made creel circa 1850. This creel has a wooden top and bottom with heavy leather front and back.

The first angling or sporting tradition came to us from the English. That tradition was not really established here until there was a class of citizen who could afford the time to be sportsmen. Their rods, reels, flies, nets and gaffs, costumes and creels were English.

Richard Leakey said the concept of a container altered the lifestyle of our ancestors. Since the first two tools were a digging stick and a container to hold many small gathered items, basketry could indeed be man's oldest form of handmade tool. With its invention, no longer would food have to be consumed on site, but could be carried home to be shared.

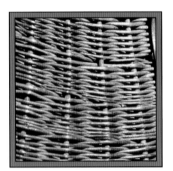

Wicker willow

Since vegetable matter is not sturdy enough to last for the many thousands of years necessary to prove anthropologists' theories, we must look to a later time for samples of this early craft. Mats, baskets, and woven fish traps are all known tools of the Neolithic and perhaps even earlier societies. The word basket itself is thought to be of Pict origin and was carried to Rome by the returning Legions. Baskets became a prized decor item in Roman households.

Both old and modern basket makers have used natural materials to build their containers. Creel makers in general have followed suit although there are several post-World War II examples in this book made of woven aluminum splints.

Checkerwork birchbark

There are two types of willow grown specifically for basketry: almond leafed willow and osier willow. Coarse baskets are made using osier willow while finer work is made by splitting willow into splints. Other materials used include split bamboo, which is very important in basketry as it is available in all warm countries. Rattan from the jungles of the Far East is one of the most popular materials because it is light, strong and flexible. Round or flat split, it is gathered, its leaves stripped, then the rattan is graded and tied into bundles by size: the smallest diameter—size one—being the most valuable. Palm fronds and other parts of various palms, split ash, oak, bass and other trees, bark and roots, are all basket making material. The materials are either woven or coiled to shape the basket. The coiled basket is constructed of bundles of material joined by stitching.

A Jicarilla Apache creel showing fine rod coiled basket making techniques.

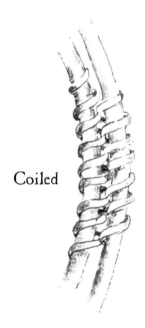

Coiled

Sometimes the bundles are coils of grass, and sometimes the bundles are replaced with a rod or several rods, but the basket is still joined by stitching. The Indians of the Southwest—Arizona, New Mexico, southern Colorado and Utah—made creels that are coiled, as are the Northwest Coast baskets.

Wicker creel from England circa 1840. This early creel has long brass hinges
running down the back as well as an impressive brass strap and latch.

The woven basket is twined, twilled, webbed, wickerworked, or checkerworked. Checkerwork is where the warp (vertical) and the weft (horizontal) are the same width, thickness and flexibility. The classic creel was generally constructed in the wickerwork method where there is an inflexible warp and flexible weft. An early French design utilized a split material for the weft, increasing its flexibility. The split willow creels could be woven tightly and became known as French weave creels. Many of the creels were sold in England, but Japanese creel makers began producing large quantities in the late 19th century and became the dominant source of French weave creels. Most of the beautiful American leathered creels were originally French weave baskets from Asia.

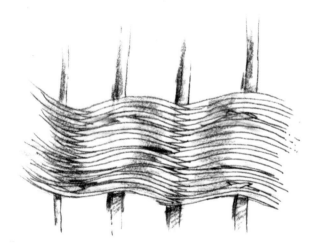

French weave

A French weave creel as it was woven in Japan around 1900, and a similar creel after it was leathered in the U.S.

The preparing and use of the material before weaving varies with the geographic location of the basket maker. For example, the Native American Algonquin used small ash logs. These billets were beaten to loosen the strips along the growth rings and then split away from the log. The strips were then trimmed for width and smoothness, using a bent knife much like farriers used in shoeing horses. The finished splints were rolled and stored for future use. In other geographic areas the splints could be made of oak. Ash and oak were ideal for making splints because they were slow growing hardwoods that provided very thin yet strong splints.

Asian bamboo was split with a tool that was driven down through the round. The blades of the tool cut the bamboo into the proper width. The pith center was removed and the splints stored wet until needed. This process was much like that used by modern cane fishing rod makers.

This checkerwork creel is made of fairly rough splints. The top is bound in a leather-like material also used for the hinges.

Young, tender, second growth willow shoots were cut, stripped of their bark, and stored in bundles until needed. Sometimes the willow was debarked by forcing each shoot through a hole in a metal plate to make uniform size splints. Some American Indians chewed the willow to remove the bark. Each material needed to be handled or worked in its own way.

Most of the production creels are wickered; that is, woven with an inflexible warp and a flexible weft. The early catalogs, both English and American, offer the creels as made of "second growth French willow" or "Asian rattan." It is certain that local makers used local materials.

Some of the local materials used were indigenous wood. Folk art creels were made of wood with drainage holes cut into the container to prevent dry rot in the wood and to allow the air to circulate. Holes were not required when oak slats were used. Oak produces a very usable and collectable creel that has better air circulation than any of the willow or rattan products.

The shape of the creel probably evolved with use. The curve of the inside surface was designed to fit the curve of the body. The placement of the hole was for easy access. The overall design was practical for the carrying of extra gear in addition to the catch of the day.

Cedar creel made with leather, fish-shaped hinges. The style is reminiscent of an old sap bucket from New England.

Wooden creel with beautiful rounded front, small holes for drainage, and a leather flap to keep the fish from jumping out of the hole in the top.

Generally the form of the creel was standard: a flat bottomed, curved basket that had a lid with an entrance hole for the angler to place the fish and an attachment for carrying a harness of some sort. Some of the early 20th century baskets had the hole in the center of the lid, but soon this changed and the hole was moved to one side or the other depending on the user—left side for the right-hander, right side for the left-hander. Since most fishermen are right-handed, you will find most creels have a left side hole. Creels with right side holes are very rare. Some creels had the hole in the side of the basket, and a few had no hole at all!

The makers (or weavers) of baskets provided a product that could be used as is. The delivered creel had a hinged lid with an opening and two holes in the back for the shoulder straps, but the harness was not included. The harness was generally sold as an accessory by the reseller or the leatherer. In the American West, many creels were reinforced with leather before being sold to the consumer. Many small saddle shops and makers of leather goods leathered a creel or two for a very good customer. There are English creels that are leathered, as were Asian creels after the second World War. Many of the European and Asian creels were purchased and sold, leathered or not, in the United States.

Fascinating wood slat creel. The center hole has a lid with a latch. (Could you get your hand into the creel?) It uses brass screws and hinges and has holes drilled in the bottom for additional drainage.

2

Western Indian Creels

This Salish creel is a great example of the art of imbrication.

Some of the most astonishing creels were made by Indian tribes of North America's West Coast ranging from the Eskimo in Alaska to the Apache in the Southwest. In the far North of Alaska, the Eskimo men, rather than the women, wove baskets of baleen, which is the flap in the upper jaw of the whale used to strain the small krill whales feed upon. The baleen was cut into splints and then twined into lovely containers that were generally topped with an ivory carving. Here we have represented a baleen creel that is one of the rarest of all creel finds. The hinges and the hasp are of ivory gathered by local hunters as they pursued the walrus.

Alaskan Eskimo made, this magnificent baleen basket was actually used as a creel many years ago.

This Salish creel is
particularly rare because of
the human figure.

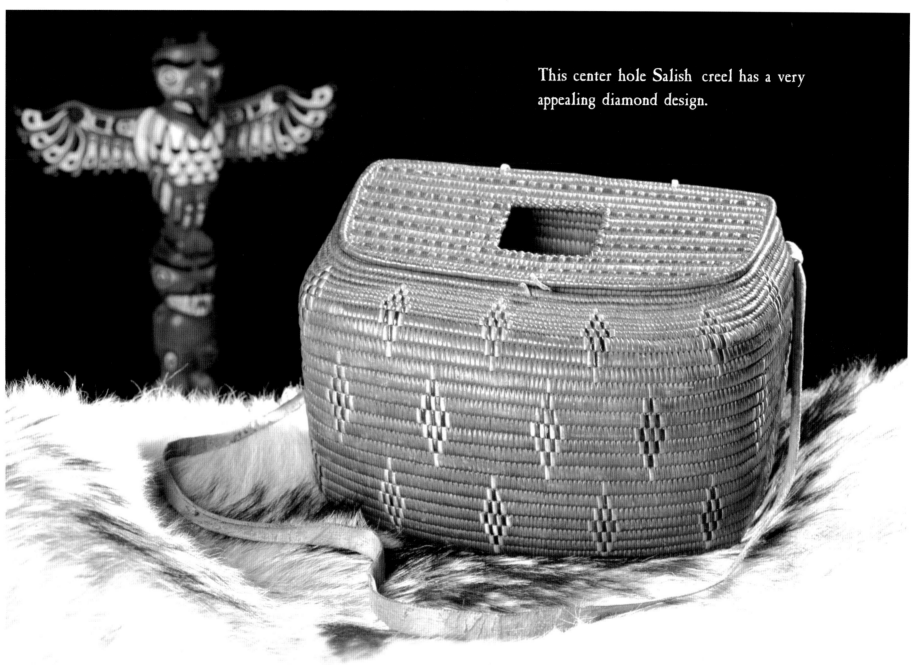

This center hole Salish creel has a very appealing diamond design.

Early in the 20th century only a very small group of collectors appreciated Indian baskets as an art form and seriously collected them. These collectors convinced some of New York's Third Avenue dealers to search out and stock pieces of tribal art. Only then were a number of private collectors and dealers able to see the artistic drama inherent in the specimens they collected. These collectors chose pieces the *makers* cared about. They allowed the makers to judge their own work which made it possible for collectors to preserve the masterworks. Another fifty years had to pass before the creel would gain this same stature. Today, authentic Indian baskets are one of the most prized types of North American folk art. Even now, few basket collectors realize that Indians made fishing creels.

This 18-inch Salish creel was probably designed for salmon or steelhead.

It is probable that the English sports fishermen in British Columbia near the end of the 19th century needed replacements for their creels and realized that local craftspeople could duplicate their European counterparts. As the weavers made creels for the trade, they adopted the form for their own use.

Unusual imbricated designs cover this coiled creel from the Pacific Northwest.

This Salish creel could have originated along the Pacific Coast between the mouth of the Columbia River and the Olympic Peninsula. It is rare to find any creel with a hole on the right side.

An early 1890-1910 Lillooet creel, this basket was woven by a woman who lived up country along the Lillooet River in British Columbia.

This Klickitat creel is owned by the University of Oregon Museum of Natural History.

This Klickitat-made creel came with a multicolored handspun, handwoven, woolen harness. Both creel and harness date near the turn of the century.

Pre-1900, this Salish creel came from a basket collector at an Indian trading post on the Thompson River.

Some of the very finest examples of Indian basketry are the Pacific Northwest's imbricated coiled creels. Imbrication is the addition of decoration to the coiling by laying a colored element on the top of each coil stitch, and then fastening each colored element in place by folding it under the next stitch. The material used to imbricate can be cherry bark, cedar or grass. A few of the early creels that follow could have been the very objects made for the European anglers.

Linked diamonds show the skill of the weaver who did extra work adding the imbrication to this creel.

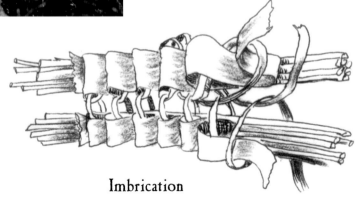

Imbrication

The name "Salish" covers a large area and includes many tribal groups. The known cultural groups that wove creels in the Pacific Northwest were the Skokomish along with the Makah, the Callam, the Nootka, the Quileute and others who lived on the Olympic Peninsula, even as far as Vancouver Island. The Klickitat and Chinook lived "over the mountains" along the Columbia River. The Lillooet and the Chilcotin were from the river areas in British Columbia that bear their names. The Fraser and Thompson River Indians also were given the names of their river homes. The Thompsons came from the mouth of the Thompson River at the Fraser River, while the Fraser people lived along their river close to the coast.

A beautiful Salish creel with two rows of imbrication.

A creel made by one of the Salish people, this was a well traveled basket that was collected in the Southwest.

The Nootka lived on the southwestern corner of Vancouver Island where they were known to have created baskets of this type.

This Thompson River creel was found by Goodwill Industries and turned over to the Burke Museum at the University of Washington.

Courtesy of the Burke Museum of
National History and Culture.
Catalog No. 1905

Collected in 1932 by Mrs. Thomas Burke, the creel above was made and used on the Fraser River of British Columbia. It is now in the Thomas Burke Museum at the University of Washington.

Courtesy of the Burke Museum of
National History and Culture.
Catalog No. 816

This Klickitat creel is a coiled basket with an unusual top. A
white deer skin thong has been woven, net like, to prevent the fish
from flopping out.

A Northeastern Maidu creel
from the Sierra Valleys north
of Lake Tahoe, this example is
false embroidered, not
imbricated.

From the Klamath River area,
this creel shows fine design
using Tule fiber.

A Yosemite area creel, this beauty is Western Paiute, probably from Mono Lake.

A Mono Lake Paiute fish basket is shown here and is a complete creel. Single rod coiled, it is of the finest workmanship. The fastener for the top is a catch from an old pair of overshoes. It is a pity that we cannot identify the weaver, because she was a master at her craft.

As recently as 1880, the natives of Yosemite National Park refused to sell their baskets to the tourists that came to visit. This soon changed, and by the turn of the century, baskets could be bought directly from the Mono Lake Paiute, the Yosemite Miwok, or maybe the Washoe women who came to the valley to trade with the tourists. Basketry soon became a part of their cash income. The designs woven into the baskets made for tribal use were changed to appeal more to the tourist who shopped in the traders' stores. Even the shapes and some of the materials changed. Beads were added to the design elements, and some of the shapes became extremely complex and difficult.

By 1916, Yosemite was holding the Indian Field Days; a rodeo and fair established to attract tourists to the park. Many of the native men labored on road crews while the women worked as maids in the hotels, but the women still wove baskets for the trade. These Field Days revived the native arts and crafts, but did not add much to the already hybridized styles. At this point, we have found only two of the surviving baskets from the fairs that show a creel-like form — a Miwok creel in the Yosemite Museum and a Western Mono in a private collection. The Mono has glass beads worked into the design.

A diagonally twined basket, this Western Mono creel has glass beads in the design. With it is a Sierra Miwok woven of split bull pine shoots.

There are also later western American Indian creels made in the classic shape with classic materials. In 1948, a six year old was given an Indian made creel by his father who had asked a friend to make it for him. Lizzi Smith, a Yurok who lived at Moreck, California, downstream on the Klamath River from Martin's Ferry, made the basket of willow and five finger fern. This wickerwork basket has leather hinges and a side hole in the oval shaped top. She made the holes in the back that would have held the harness.

The Jicarilla Apache of the Southwest coiled excellent creels. There are four coiled baskets shown in this chapter. The shape is classic creel: bulbous, larger at the bottom than at the top and with a very

This delightful little willow creel was woven for a little boy by Lizzie Smith, a Yurok Indian on the Hupa Reservation just after World War II.

generous indentation for the curve of the body. The finishing row at the top of the creel is typical of Apache work. The use of colored coils to create designs is also featured. The design elements appear to be fish, birds and other animals. The Apache creels are decorated in typical fashion with the fish, the Thunderbird, geometric designs and the "Nohokos" - a Navaho word for the rolling log design that was later hijacked by Nazi Germany and called the "Swastika." The sun has faded the dyes on the outside, but the inside of many creels remains bright.

Jicarilla Apache woven, this Thunderbird creel, while faded from the light on the outside, is bright and colorful on the inside.

The Jicarilla Apache featured this bulbous shape and a curved back in many of the creels they wove.

All of the baskets in this chapter were made west of the Rockies or in the Southwest and are masterworks deserving to be treated as the finest of American folk art. As the presence of these historically and culturally important folk art specimens become more widely appreciated, their cultural as well as historical value will grow.

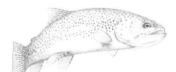

This Jicarilla Apache creel features the Nohokos design of the Navaho.

This is a larger example of the traditional Jicarilla design.

3

Eastern Woodland Creels

The creels that are most thought of as "Indian" are those fabricated east of the Mississippi. The Iroquois, Chippewa, Menominees, Algonquin, Ojibwas and other Eastern Woodland tribes used oak, ash, birch and other white wood splints to make plain in-and-out checkerwoven baskets.

The Eastern Woodland Indian creels pose a problem in identification. Because the materials and the methods used are the same, very few, if any, of the ethnologists can tell the difference between the makers, be they Native American or European-American. The probable reason is that by the time the ethnologists and the anthropologists got around to studying the Woodland natives, the Native Americans had to a large degree been assimilated into the social structure of the Eastern United States and Canada. Eastern Indian creels and those creels made in this style are thus all grouped together as Woodland splint creels.

One of the finest examples to surface is the very warm ash splint creel that begins this chapter. It is a superb example of Woodland Indian work. There is little doubt about its origin. The owner collected it from the maker's family in the Greenville, Maine area.

Checkerwork

Classic splint creel with carved wooden center hole. The hinges and latch are also splint with a wood carved latch pin. Believed to be a Maine Indian creel, it was collected in Greenville, Maine.

A spectacular splint creel with rectangular bottom tapering to an oval top. The top has twisted splints for design. The creel was made in the Great Lakes area and is shown with a knife used to make this kind of splint.

Wide diagonal checkwork splints give the creel a different look. The hole is along the back hinge, and the latch is a wooden knob fastened to the inside of the basket's front.

Some Woodland splint creels were tall and thin while others were short and long in design. The tall one shown is from Maine. The diagonal weave catches the eye of the collector as most Woodlands-made creels had a rather straightforward look about them.

The vertical wooden latch woven into the front of this splint creel is a fairly common solution to the problem of how to fasten down the lid.

A Maine Indian creel with a small hole. This tall, slender creel exhibits excellent craftsmanship.

Sometimes the skill of the Adirondack basket maker carried over to other objects. He or she might make a net to go with the guide's creel. Variations in the design could include partitions to separate the fish from the gear and the use of leather straps to add strength.

The finders of these Eastern Woodland creels hunted them from the northeastern provinces of Canada down into the Carolinas, and there is no area of consistency in size for either the creels or the weaver splints. Large and small splints were used by all of the makers to vary design.

A side hole creel from upstate New York. The creel also has dividers inside to separate gear from fish. The net was made by the creelmaker.

Many creels have wooden lids that make the lid sturdier and are easier to construct. Note the metal loops on the lid for attaching the shoulder strap.

This creel features a lid with wider splints than in the front. Note also the classic carved wooden center hole.

A good number of these creels were finished with a hoop of wood at the top and a lid. Some of the lids were solid wood, while others were woven splints. Some lids had metal hinges attached to the wooden hoop, but almost all of them had holes to receive the fish. Some were so large as to require straps to sling the basket like a backpack, or as the English called them, a pannier. Here again, interest was created by varying the widths of the woof and weft elements.

This small creel has a lid with a double wooden rim fastened together with brass tacks. The weaving is tight and the color of the splints has a great patina.

The lid on this creel was rounded by hand, the wooden latch and clasp are also handmade. This small creel has loops on the front for a jacket, etc., as there is not much space inside.

A beautiful wooden lid and a bulbous basket makes this a classic Woodland splint creel.

Latching the lid remains a problem on splint creels. This maker solves the problem by attaching a leather thong diagonally across the lid to serve as a hinge and loop to latch onto the vertical wooden catch.

Bulbous shape, tight weaving, and hand made lid make this creel a great example of splint creels.

The examples illustrated show some of the variations on this theme. Because basketry was a major source of income for the Native Americans, shapes and sizes varied according to the demands of the trade. These Native American basket makers were the leaders in the field. The commercial makers that supplied L.L. Bean also used native methods.

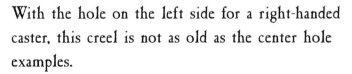

With the hole on the left side for a right-handed caster, this creel is not as old as the center hole examples.

By twisting and weaving additional splints onto the front of this creel, the maker created an unusual and very appealing design.

A one-inch diameter stick provides structure for the lid, the basket and a place to attach the shoulder strap on this circa 1920 creel.

Another very interesting shape of creel is known as the Watermelon. Found all over
the country, they were woven of grape vines, oak splints and even willow.

This watermelon creel features a
wooden door and black paint and
exemplifies the variety of designs
in creels.

A wire frame is used to shape this
unusual watermelon creel with brass
fittings and a spring-loaded metal
door for the fish.

An old birchbark creel painted with folk art flowers dates back to the early 1900s.

Eastern Woodland Indians also made baskets and creels out of birch bark.

In only a few cases are the makers known. The birchbark creel made in 1926 by George Baker is of a single piece of bark wrapped front to back. George lived on the New York side of Lake Champlain. Other birchbark creels came from such diverse places as Minnesota and Manitoba or New York and Quebec. The skill in utilizing birch in creel making also varied. The laced and designed versions of the birchbark are certainly the most artistic – the strips of birch, plainly woven in a straight checkerwork pattern make them very appealing.

This creel is made with one piece of birch bark wrapped from front to back around the bottom. It was made by George Baker in 1926, who lived on the New York side of Lake Champlain.

A beautifully painted birchbark creel with no hole in the top. The scalloped flap is just for decoration.

This creel has a wooden top and bottom wrapped together with one piece of birch bark. It has wide pieces of leather on the sides to hold the shoulder strip.

This center hole creel has a wooden bottom with birch bark around it, but the top is lashed to an oval bent twig frame, as is the lid. The lashing is intricate and the straps and hinges are made of leather.

A birchbark creel from Minnesota, supposedly made by a Scandinavian. Note the off-center hole.

This is a classic birchbark creel with the basket made from one piece of birch bark that was cut, then folded, and finally stitched together at the ends.

From woodsplint to birch bar, the creel makers in the Eastern Section of North America provide a wide variety of artistically appealing creels.

4

George Lawrence Co. Creels

When the angler left the spring creeks of the east and moved west to the freestone rivers, the need for added reinforcement was realized. Climbing the rocky banks, busting through the brush, willows and quaking aspens all put extraordinary strain on the corners, the hinges and the tops of a creel. A frugal western fisherman would take his creel to the local saddle shop and the artisans there would reinforce it with leather.

Leather reinforced creels have a long history in the United Kingdom. In fact, Scotland's McPhearson was already using leather to reinforce creels in 1884. It was in the American West, however, that this form of the creel reached its apex. Oregon was the center of the leathered creel business.

The most important leatherer of creels in Oregon was the George Lawrence Company. Lawrence set the standard for leather reinforced fish baskets. Every leathered creel is measured against Lawrence's. George Lawrence's great grandson, Bill Lawrence III writes:

> "The company was established by my great grandfather's brother in law, Sam Sherlock. Sam, after working in the saddlery trade in the northeastern United States, came to Oregon via the Isthmus of Panama. After arrival in Portland, Oregon, Sherlock established a livery stable and harness supply business in 1857. In 1873, George W. Lawrence joined Sam in the Sherlock saddle and harness business. After Sam's death that same year, George L. ran the business for the widow. In 1893, with the minor financial interests of his three sons, (George, John and my grandfather, William), George, Sr. bought out the Sherlock interests and changed the name to The Geo. Lawrence Co.

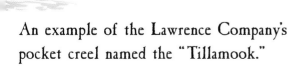

An example of the Lawrence Company's pocket creel named the "Tillamook."

A rare early Lawrence creel with designs cut out of the leather. It was custom-made in the "Walton" style.

In 1903, after being located in at least two other places near the waterfront in downtown Portland, my great grandfather built a four story building on the southeast corner of S.W. First and Oak streets for the manufacture and sale in the west to the trade (dealers and other saddle and harness shops) of saddlery and harness and the components and hardware that it took to make them. In the early days the Geo. Lawrence factory was famous on the west coast as 'the white factory' because of the bright appearance of its whitewashed brick and beam interior in contrast to the normally dirty condition of most harness and saddle operations of the time. One floor was devoted to saddlery manufacturing and one to harness making. There was a great rivalry between the men who worked with harness leather making horse harness and related items and the strap leather workers who made saddles and the rest of the strap goods, and that rivalry was not always friendly."

The historically designated Lawrence building stands today, restored as an office building. It still gives testimony to its illustrious past.

The "Hazeldell" had a single leather strap running around the creel and no embossing. It is usually marked with a "D."

Bill Lawrence III, at the sewing machine, used to sew leather onto creels. He is holding a "Hazeldell" creel.

The Lawrence Co. first applied leather to split-willow creels, which were woven in the French weave style and imported from Japan. The leathering was uncomplicated. First covering about half of the top with leather, they then added the strap, or the end of the strap, binding the edge with leather while using the binding to anchor the top leather. The strap was then riveted through the edge of the lid. A buckle was finally added to the body unless pockets interfered, and then the strap and buckle were reversed. This method remained constant throughout all the years of production and may help in identifying special order and unmarked Lawrence creels.

This creel is marked "3D" indicating the Hazeldell model. Note the loop at the back of the lid.

Looking through the old Lawrence catalogs, one can see the progression of their creel business. The 1923 issue noted, "We leather fish baskets at reasonable price(s)," and offered "fish basket straps" in several widths and qualities. The first offer of a finished leathered creel came in a mailer sent in 1924. This creel had the edges of the top leather embossed as was the center body strip.

Embossing was the rolling of a wheel of metal across the leather. Under pressure, the wheel left an impression or design on the surface of the leather. Stamping was another method of imparting a design onto the leather, but it was hand work, done one impression at a time. Tooling, or "hand carved," as cowboys called it, meant using a knife or other hand tool to cut a decorative design into the leather.

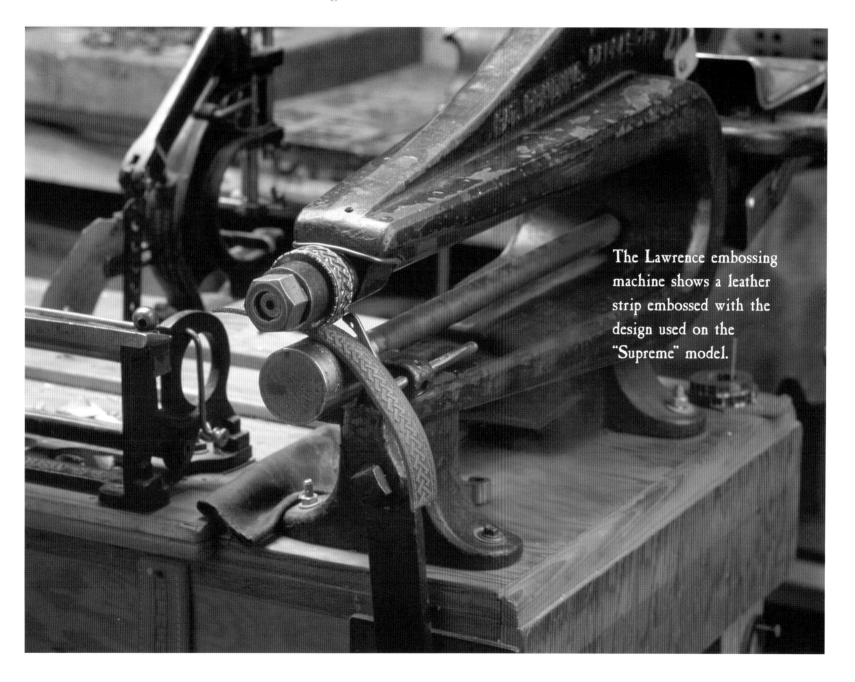

The Lawrence embossing machine shows a leather strip embossed with the design used on the "Supreme" model.

Four popular sizes of that first Lawrence leathered creel were presented:

NUMBER	SIZE	CAPACITY
No. 3	14 inches	20 pounds
No. 4	15 inches	25 pounds
No. 5	16 inches	30 pounds
No. 6	17 inches	35 pounds

These sizes and capacities remained constant and the numbers represent the industry standard for sizing creels. In early advertising the Lawrence Co. emphasized visual appeal.

"While I don't know the genesis of the leathered creel with the Geo. Lawrence Co., my research shows that it first appeared in the 1923 catalog and was last shown in 1953. Normally a product would be introduced and sold for a while before it was seen in a catalog. This process ensured its success. I also suspect that there wasn't much honor among competitors and that if the Lawrence Company came up with a good idea, one of our several competitors in Portland would jump on the bandwagon as soon as they saw it in the catalog, and visa versa."

"The sight of a Lawrence fish basket creates a desire to own one"

The "Supreme" from George Lawrence. More of this model were produced than any other.

The "Lowboy" by George Lawrence. This creel used "Supreme" embossing and is fairly rare.

These two "Lowboys" are very rare, particularly the large "Size 6" with a custom pocket and harness.

By 1929, the single style had grown to at least six different styles, then two more sizes were added—the "Number 7", an eighteen-incher with a forty-pound capacity; and the "Number 2," a thirteen-inch, fifteen-pounder. This was the year that the metal cartouche was also added. During the early years, leather had been stamped to indicate the maker. Now there were several different stamps used during production.

The creels could be stained before the leather was sewn on, as illustrated by this green "Supreme."

Each of these styles had a number and/or a letter that indicated the style and size. The first style had just a single digit number to indicate the size. Now a letter or additional numbers were added. A twenty-pound "Number 3" creel became a "Number 3A." The double pocket creel was known as a "304" in the twenty-five-pound capacity, or "305" in the thirty-pounder. The plain, unleathered basket carried just the old single digit. After the digit, "AL" indicated the "Lowboy" style with "Supreme" leathering. They asked $1.00 a basket extra to color them in natural willow, mission oak, red, green or blue. After a year or so, the price dropped to fifty cents. Varnish was added after coloring. At other times, it was noted that shellac was used on the creels. Also, the shoulder straps were sold separately and came in various types including a harness that wrapped around the creel.

Rare Lawrence creel with zipper, pocket, buckstitching, and no embossing. This creel is marked with the G.L.C.O. diamond mark (rare for creels, common for saddles and chaps).

"I can understand how the leathered creel business would be desirable for a shop like ours. First of all, the leather used for the corner, edges and flaps would probably be called scrap leather and come from the belly part of the side of leather. Leather from the belly is looser grained than from the back of the shoulder and, therefore, works better when moulding to the shape of those areas of the creel. Besides, leather used at those locations on the baskets didn't have to be strong. It just had to look good. On the other hand, the leather used for pouches or where the embossed design is placed must be of a firmer quality so that the embossing process won't distort or cut the leather, and the embossed impression will be deep and sharp."

The "Rainbow" featured lots of leather, two pockets, and no embossing.

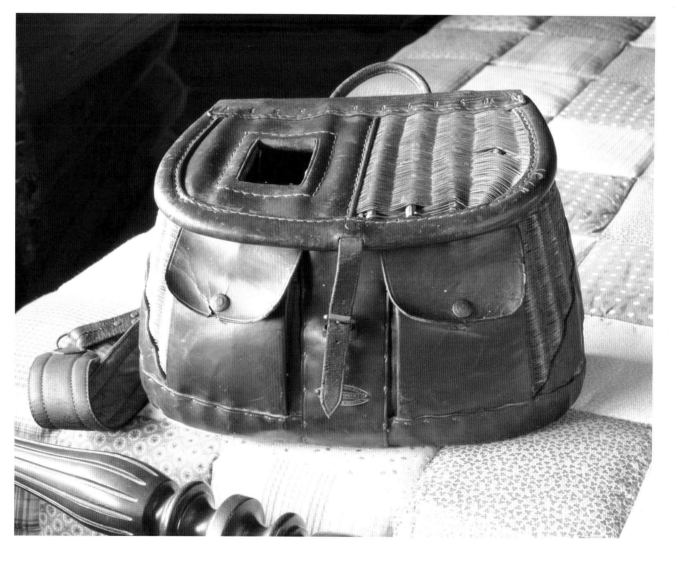

In 1931, the creel designs took names rather than just numbers. The "300s" had the added name of the "Rainbow," while the "400s" became known as the "Walton." There were also the "Tillamook," the "Lowboy" and the "Supreme." By 1932, the names were gone from the catalogs, although collectors still refer to the creels by name, and 1941 saw whole willow wickerweave creels (Number 14X) added to the list. These were noted as being made in China.

A classic
Tillamook, this
creel shows
another variation
in the shape of
the pocket.

An early center hole
Lawrence embossed with the
supreme design.

"I was told that in 1942 most of the leathering of creels was done by Oscar Simon."

Leathering had gone from a whole department down to just one man. In the glory days, one could find at least 10 different Lawrence styles available.

"The basic leather used was vegetable tanned strap leather. As opposed to chrome tanned leather, vegetable tannage could be worked damp with water. It was the addition of just the right amount of moisture that was the key to successfully forming and stamping and tooling the strap leather. The final treatment was the neatsfoot oil compound that set the final molded shape and tooling and gave the product the final rich red "Lawrence" brown color. Filling the leather fibers with the oil helped prevent water from penetrating the leather and undoing the shape of the mold or the depth of the tooling.

Custom made Lawrence with fish on the lid using a chain pattern embossing wheel. This creel was leathered with Cordovan (horsehide) rather than the standard cowhide.

The creel harness was sold separately. This harness was also custom-fitted with a sheath for a fishing knife.

The G. L. Co. always offered custom order service. Because of this, there may be any number of Lawrence creels that might have unique features requested by a customer; from "no maker name" to custom tooling, accessory items or other special requests.

Several unmarked creels with Lawrence-style construction have been found and collected. They are generally thought to be Lawrence-made.

We have found many Lawrence-like creels that were probably made by Lawrence for someone else and stamped with the customer's name. Marshall Wells was such a customer.

"Fasteners from the rattan and willow creels that the Geo. Lawrence Co. got from the Orient were removed to allow for the leathering operation. The metal name plates that were riveted to most creels, hardware for the straps used to tether live duck decoys, buckles and hardware for the fish baskets along with the embossing wheels that put the design into the leather panels on the creels and creel straps are all stored in my workplace.

This creel marked "Marswell" for Marshall Wells Hardware store in Oregon shows classic Lawrence construction, while using an embossing design seen only on "Marswell" creels.

Lawrence sold the plain unleathered baskets as well. The prices in Lawrence catalogs were at least 65% less than the leathered creels. Of course, the shoulder straps were sold separately.

Center-hole creel in the Lawrence shop with many varieties of buckles that were removed after the baskets came from Asia to be leathered.

Later Lawrence creels with whole willow baskets (rather than French weave) and the "Supreme" embossing.

These quotations from the memoirs of W.C. (Bill) Lawrence III, George Lawrence's great grandson, provide insight into the early days of the harness and saddlery business. Bill started with the company in 1957,

"...its centennial year, and ran the leather goods factory for about thirty years. We made mostly leather shooting accessories, holsters, belts, scabbards, rifle slings, etc. ... using the same techniques and machinery from the early saddlery making years of the company."

This 14X creel is one of the last models made by the Geo. Lawrence Co.

After being disabled with a spinal cord disease, Bill retired and the family sold the company. Bill retained some of the old equipment and the embossing wheels used to decorate saddles, cuffs and spur leathers. Today he uses the machines to do some repair, restoration and reproduction work as well as to create several unique leathergood items. Write to Bill Lawrence at 4838 S.W. 19th Drive, Portland, OR 97201. You may call him at 503-246-9922.

The last Lawrence catalog that showed creels (1952) listed a whole rattan basket, "Number 10," leathered, without pocket and a "10P" with pocket. There still was a split willow, as the "Number 12" was the old "Supreme," but the "12P" had a pocket in front. The great variety, however, was gone.

That was the end of the manufacturing and leathering of fishing creels, but not the end of Lawrence, the King of the Creel Leatherers. Today, as far as the creel collector is concerned, a Lawrence is the "coin of the realm."

This example of one of the last embossed Lawrence creel designs from the early 1950s shows how they were getting away from the "Supreme" embossing.

McMonies Creels

McMonies creels are superbly leathered and visually stunning. The quality of the baskets, the coloring and the leatherwork all combine with the highest quality craftsmanship to make them beautiful and desirable works of art.

W. H. McMonies & Co was one of Portland's fine harness makers. They were famous for their horse collars which were even sold to the Lawrence Company for resale. Bill Lawrence III is very specific in paying tribute to the McMonies Harness Company.

The McMonies buckstitching as seen on the mint brown "Lowboy" is far superior to any other maker's, and they were the first to add zippers to the tops and pockets. It would seem that this addition would give a bulky or heavy appearance to the creel, but this is not so. McMonies' design and method of sewing, as well as their choice of zippers, add to the balance of the creel. The buckstitching draws the eye and contributes to the overall beauty of the McMonies product. Brown, red, and green were the colors that the McMonies artists used on the creel to balance the creative leather work and this puts their creels at the top of the collector's wish list.

McMonies measuring device for horse collars.

Rare McMonies Lowboy exhibiting all the great McMonies features.

McMonies stained its baskets in various colors like Lawrence. This nearly
mint-condition creel was stained red before the leather was applied.

Buckstitching is done by hand. The leatherworker punches a hole in the leather and threads a leather lace through to the other side and then punches another hole to lace back to the original side. Fine quality buckstitching requires the hole to be the same size as the lace. As one saddlemaker put it,

"Buckstitching a creel has got to be a real pain." Since you cannot punch wicker without breaking it, the leather must be punched before it is sewn on the creel and then an awl must be used to part the wicker as the leather is laced through each hole.

How about a green McMonies? This stained creel also features the famous buckstitching and "snake" embossing design.

Classic McMonies with a spectacular design on the front zippered pocket.

McMonies put different designs on the front pocket, including this lucky horseshoe and four leaf clover.

Instead of being dipped in stain before
leathering, this creel was "painted"
green with a brush.

This McMonies creel has straps and buckles to fasten the lid and a pocket instead of a zipper.

The color was added to the creel before leathering. While earlier baskets were painted with a dull finish, the latter ones have a lovely patina, the result of a newer process of applying color as well as a change in the quality and mixture of the paint.

While some of the pockets are plain, others are stamped with a very interesting design. The embossing that appears on all of the higher grade McMonies creels shows patterns not seen on other makers' creels. The wheels that carried the embossing designs were offered in great variety, although few saddleries bought them all. McMonies took advantage of these offerings and must have purchased many for we have found creels with a twined basket weave, others with a running "s" and still others that have a chain pattern. All this leads to the assumption that McMonies was a custom house as far as creel leathering was concerned. There are very few McMonies creels that are alike.

The story of the classic McMonies top so far, is that there is no *one* McMonies top. Each seems to be slightly different from the others. But the basic method of applying the leather was always the same: half of the top was covered with an embossed piece of leather that had the hole area pre-cut. The leather at the top and bottom edge of the hole was turned under then stitched, or buckstitched, as the case may be, around the hole along the center edge. The edging leather was then stretched into place and the top and the edge were stitched together to the top. If the creel was to have a zipper, the edging leather was left loose at the bottom, and the top edge of the zipper was fastened to it. Zipper or not, the inside top edge of the basket also had a leather edging to protect it. The variety could be seen in which embossing and/or stamping were used and how the buckles and straps were attached.

You will find great variation in the leather finish and color of McMonies creels, as shown by this dark leather model.

How unusual to find red glass studs on a McMonies strap and creel. This one is basket-stamped, buckstitched and has no zippers. Like all the others, it appears to be unique.

This creel has no pocket and is similar to a Lawrence except for the "snake" embossing and the McMonies plate on the back.

The "snake" embossing is used to form a beautiful rectangular design on this McMonies.

Most McMonies creels are marked with a metal name plate fastened to the back of the leather hinge. The name was spelled differently in the two styles of metal plates used. One plate is lettered "MC MONIES HAND MADE IN THE WEST PORTLAND, ORE." and the other "MACMONIES HAND MADE PORTLAND, ORE." There are also some creels with "McMonies" stamped into the leather on the back of the creel or under the flap of the pocket. The same leather stamp is found on shoulder harnesses and on other items such as cartridge belts.

There are at least three different model numbers found on the back of McMonies creels. Model #80s are creels with zippered lids and pockets, Model #60s and #65s are creels with pockets but no zippers, and Model #50s are creels without pockets or zippers. The size is also frequently marked on the back using a "4" or "5," etc. Some wicker creels have also been found with McMonies-marked shoulder straps and with the original Asian lid strap and hinge replaced with heavier leather pieces. Note that within each model number there were great variations as to embossing and decoration.

The lists of saddle makers from the western collectable scene document both a W. H. McMonies and an A. E. McMonies actively engaged in

This creel exhibits another McMonies embossing wheel that looks like a basket weave design.

the leather goods business in Portland, Oregon. They did not produce the great number of creels that Lawrence did, but the creels they did produce were of the highest quality and many people today consider the McMonies to be *the* artists of the creel leatherers.

This McMonies uses a whole willow creel. It does have a zipper and very nice buckstitching.

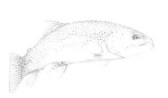

McMonies also sold wicker creels that were basically unleathered except for a McMonies strap and a heavy lid strap and buckle.

Clark Creels

The John Clark Saddlery Co. was probably the first major Oregon saddle company to begin leathering creels. John Clark started the company in 1878. He died in 1923 and his family kept the company going until 1927.

The vast majority of Clark creels are unmarked. The confusion over which Clark produced the creels is cleared up by the green creel that starts this chapter. The small snap is stamped with the John Clark Saddlery marking that is found on many saddles and pairs of chaps.

There is a lack of consistency in the design of the decoration, and there was much more hand stamping than embossing on Clark creels. Clark also used both plain and harness buckles (buckles with a loop on the buckle prong). Frequently, Clark creels used a horizontal strap below the buckle for added strength.

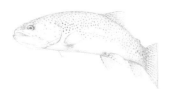

The exceptional creel has a snap on
the lid bearing the Clark logo.

One of the most complicated of leather constructions is featured on this
Clark creel. The hinge, lid design and lid edge binding are all one piece of
leather. Similarly, only one piece of leather was used on the back, sides and
front, including the binding at the top edge of the basket itself.

Clark's creelwork differs from the Lawrence in the way the leather was applied. Clark first bound half of the top's edge, then inserted the strap for the buckle through the edge binding, stitching it above the binding with either a cross or a box, finally adding a rivet placed through the strap and edge for security. The hole side of the top was then covered with a leather piece and turned under the rest of the top's edge. In many of the Clark creels the only true consistency is in the way the top leather has been added. This lack of uniformity can be blamed, perhaps, on the possibility that more than one person leathered the creels purported to be Clark's. Since there was no machine work, the variability of hand stitching would seem to support this hypothesis, as do the variations in the stamping. There are long stitches, short stitches, double waxed linen threads and single threads.

Classic Clark hand-stamping is shown on this creel. The basket has a slanted bottom and top typical of some early French weave baskets.

Early on, it appears that the Clark creels were hand-stamped with many different patterns.

The lid strap on Clark creels is fastened by running the strap through the lid rim binding and sewing the top end of the strap to the creel behind the rim binding.

Due to the great variety and early style of construction, Clark creels are very interesting and collectable.

On a Clark creel, the leather piece covering half of the lid is wrapped around the edge of the lid to form the rim binding.

The 1926 Honeyman Hardware
Company Catalog #10 showed
this design and called it the
"LaBelle" model.

CHAPTER

7

Peters Creels

Golf bags and leather sporting goods were the specialties of the E. P. Peters Company of Portland, Oregon. On a 1926 calendar, they proudly promoted "Finest Hand Made" and "Totally Hand Made" leather products. The creels they made certainly fall into this category. Fortunately, a few Peters creels have survived, representing great examples of artistic achievement.

These Peters-stamped creels show superior craftsmanship, but each basket is different in its manner of design and execution. The only consistency, other than the stamp, is the buckle. Peters used the harness buckle that has a lock hole built into the tongue. Each of the Peters creels could have been a custom job for an individual angler. It could be that Peters buckstitching was so good that they did it for other makers.

The finest Peters workmanship is exhibited on this large #5-sized creel. The pocket is one of the largest of creel pockets and requires two straps.

Peters creels feature great variety. This creel has two pockets in the front, a flap over the top hole, and buckstitching.

Some Peters creels were not
heavily leathered, but they still
have appealing designs on the
leather and a common buckle.

The buckstitched Peters creels that we show here have the feeling of McMonies while the other Peters pictured seems more like a Lawrence, especially in the style and method of construction.

Unusual vertical pieces of leather on the front corners set this Peters creel apart from most other creels.

This Peters creel is constructed in the Lawrence style and leads one to believe that Peters was connected with the Lawrence Company in some way.

Most Schnell creels have a two-by-two brick design. This #5-sized creel also has a Lawrence-type harness that holds the creel.

Other Marked Leather Creels

JOSEPH SCHNELL

It would be difficult indeed to separate a Schnell from a Lawrence creel except for the rubber stamp cartouche. The construction of a Schnell is the same as that of a Lawrence. Many of the Schnells feature the same design, using a two by two brick design and buckstitching to match the color of the leather. This design is very appealing, particularly on some of the older Schnells that have a great patina.

Collectors have long thought that Joseph Schnell, of Portland, Oregon, had a connection to the Geo. Lawrence Co. His craftsmanship certainly reflected Lawrence's quality. Once again, the surmise of the collectors proves to be correct. Bill Lawrence III, while talking about his great grandfather's company was able to clear up this point. He wrote:

> "I was told by a former employee that in 1942 most of the creels were leathered by Oscar Simon. Oscar also specialized in making horse bridles in the G.L. Co.'s shop. This old timer also told me that Oscar as well as Perle Payton and Joe Schnell, G.L. Co.. saddle makers, all leathered baskets at home, peddled them around the area, and may have identified them with their own names."

This Schnell creel is distinctive because of the unusual design on the leather.

K. G. MCKEEMAN (KENNS)

Kenns was the brand name used by K. G. McKeeman. He was noted for using extra heavy leathers on his creels. While most saddle shops who leathered creels used belly leather not usuable for saddles or harnesses, McKeeman used the actual bends, or the prime leather from the hide. Two small leather hinges were added inside a long leather outer hinge that added to the sturdiness of the Kenns creel.

This Kenns creel is a little lighter and is leathered on a French weave basket.

Toward the end of Geo. Lawrence Co.'s production of creels in the 1950s, there was discussion between K. G. McKeeman and Bill Lawrence about McKeeman going to work for Lawrence, but no working relationship was formed.

Kenns creels feature heavy leather and in this case, a large pocket.

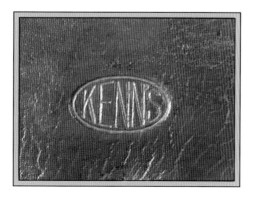

Frisbee creels
generally had no
design on the
leather and most
were made with
green-dyed whole
willow baskets.

FRISBEE

Conventional wisdom has it that Frisbee was a McMonies foreman. One collector has a McMonies cartridge belt with a Frisbee holster that matches. The two clearly worked together, but whether Frisbee made creels before or after working for McMonies is uncertain.

The best of the known Frisbee creels was purchased at Mier and Frank in Portland, Oregon, sometime during 1947. Mier and Frank had a complete fly fishing shop on the top floor of their Portland department store. Just after the new creel was taken home and before the fishing season started, the buyer passed away and his wife stored it in the attic still in its original M and F bag. After being up there for thirty or more years, a neighbor was able to purchase it from the widow.

This leather Frisbee has a plain leather pocket added to the typical Frisbee leather construction.

Nelson creels have lots of heavy leather and most feature the same interlocking scallop pattern.
This one is stamped "Meir-Frank" on the hinge.

A. E. NELSON

Now known as the A. E. Nelson Leather Company, Adelbert E. Nelson learned the leather trade in his father's harness shop in Herman, Minnesota. After a stint in a saddle shop in Montana, he moved in about 1938 to Salem, Oregon, but he didn't begin leathering creels until after World War II. His sporting products were generally sold through retailers such as Meir and Frank. Other Nelson leathered creels have been seen with cartouches such as Q's Sporting Goods, Billings, Montana, and Abercrombie & Fitch. The Nelson Company is still making leather products in Scio, Oregon, near Salem. They now specialize in hunting and law enforcement leathers. But if one wanted a creel leathered today, they could do the job.

Nelson is still producing a couple of models of creels. This one is about 5-10 years old.

Cane strips are beautifully woven to make the classic Turtle basket. Good quality leather is stamped and applied in much the same way as that done by Oregon leathersmiths. There is a great variety in the baskets themselves and they have a handcrafted feel.

TURTLE

The quality of the workmanship and the Korean-American connection have combined to make Turtle creels fascinating. They come in three general styles.

The first style is the leathered creel. The basket is made of strips of cane, the same material from which fishing rods are made. The strips of cane are woven almost checkerwork style into a fine basket. For added strength, the bottom is reinforced with a hemp cord woven in different designs. The basket is then leathered in the Western American style using a fairly good grade of cowhide. The most common mark on these leather Turtles was "Ilhan New, Boulder, Colo.," but many of the leather Turtles were not marked.

The second style uses the same cane basket, but is not leathered. Instead, a hand carved turtle is used as a latch for the lid, hence the name "Turtle" creel. The turtle is hand carved in many poses including lying on its side.

The third style is a production model of the Turtle creel using a basket made of willow instead of cane. The turtles on this creel are all the same.

The top creel is a cane creel without the leather. Instead, it has a wooden ruler along the back and a carved Turtle latch. The bottom creel is a later whole willow production creel made in Korea.

Classic example of a Frog creel, featuring diagonal straps across the front and three bands of leather running around the creel from top to bottom.

WHITNEY SPORTING GOODS CO.

Colorado has produced some interesting leathered creels. The company that was most active was the Whitney Sporting Goods Co. Early on, the company sold "leather reinforced creels of our own design using oak tanned leather." These creels have come to be known as "Frog" creels, as the two pieces cross in front of the creel like the legs of a frog. The leg straps start at the low middle of the front of the creel and curve to end just at the back edge of the creel with a ring on either side as a place to attach the shoulder harness. Consequently, the harness holes found in the back of the Asian-made baskets were not used.

The July 1939 issue of *Western Sportsman* introduced the Haywood All American Creel in an article titled "Blind Start New American Industry." Leslie B. Smith writes about how he became interested in manufacturing creels in the U.S. after learning that 99% of the fish baskets were imported from Japan. At about the same time, the Colorado State Blind Commission's broom factory was having problems being in competition with American manufacturing. After overcoming many design problems the blind workers began manufacturing the Haywood All American Fish Basket at competitive prices. The Whitney Sporting Goods Co. of Denver, Colorado, became the distributor and the creels were sold throughout America.

Another model sold by Whitney used the whole top of the leather hinge for the stamp. Called the "Haywood Fish Keeper," this creel had both the name of the store and the model name stamped into the leather in large letters.

The Haywood Fish Keeper was from Colorado and sold in the Whitney Sporting Goods store in Denver.

We'll Pay $1 For Your Dealer's Name!
...to Introduce this New American Made Creel

HAYWOOD ALL AMERICAN CREEL

MAIL THIS COUPON TODAY!

A Tufts and Lyons
marked creel with
center hole. Nicely
framed with good
quality leather, this
appears to be one of
a kind.

A whole-willow leathered creel
modified by Olsen-Nolte, who
fastened pouches onto the ends
of the creel.

CALIFORNIA

A few leathered creels have turned up with a "California" mark. For example, the cartouche of the Los Angeles-based Tufts and Lyons Arms Company was found on a center-hole leathered creel. A very tightly-woven French basket, the leathering was expertly done and covered only the center portion of the top. There was edging on the top and the lip of the basket. Corner reinforcements and a wide center strip completed the leathering.

Apparently, a one-of-a-kind creel was found in the Clear Lake region of California. The leather pockets are stamped "Olsen-Nolte, San Francisco." The Olsen-Nolte spokesman noted that the cartouche indicated that the pockets had been added some time after 1942 as the stamp used from 1938 to 1942 read "Nolte-Olsen." As Olsen-Nolte didn't normally produce leather creels, the customer had to have been someone who spent a lot of money with Olsen-Nolte because of the attitudes of the early managers and owners of the shop.

The Ellery Arms Co. of San Francisco was another purveyor of creels. They surely purchased Asian made baskets and had them leathered for sale in their place of business. We can find no mention of Ellery as a harness or saddle shop, however, so it is highly doubtful that they did their work in-house.

Ellery Arms Co. is marked on this creel. It was embossed with a common design and the leather was applied in typical western fashion.

9

Unmarked Leather Creels

The possible origins of creels leathered by "unknowns" are one of the most interesting and fun areas for the collector, because they provide a mystery that begs to be solved. In doing some detective work, one can start with the basket's shape, size, type of construction and quality of workmanship. The fasteners and hinges may also provide clues as to the time and place of manufacture. If the creel is leathered, it may be important to note how the leather is fastened to the creel, as well as how the design was applied. These creels are extremely interesting, and we can only speculate about their origins until more information becomes available.

One of the best and most skillfully wickered rattan baskets was found in Jackson Hole, Wyoming, but originated in San Francisco. There are two distinctive features to the basket itself. First, it is made of the best quality wicker, and secondly, its bulbous shape is English in style. The leather is hand-stamped, which indicates the work of early West Coast leathersmiths. These are the only clues to the mystery of this creel's origin.

This very appealing creel was produced by an unknown maker. The basket is made of top quality rattan, the leather is in the western style, while its shape may be English.

A pair of "S-embossed" creels featuring the same embossing and stitching with similar lid and
fastener construction. The main difference is that the lower creel has been "frogged."

Another mystery is a group of creels that have an "S" embossed on the leather, all of which seem to have come from the same hand. At least a dozen of these "S" creels have surfaced, but the identity of who made them has been lost. The "S" is very much like the McMonies "S" but is smaller. There are many other unknown Asian-made creels which seem to have been embossed and leathered in the United States.

The same "S" embossing and construction are used on this nice small creel. The problem is that we have no strong evidence of who made these creels.

An unknown maker went to a lot of trouble to add the design of an anchor, sailboat and a fish on the hinge of this very unique creel.

There are other creels that provide no indication of the maker's identity, but are nevertheless collectable folk art as a result of their fine craftsmanship and superior design. These are mostly one-of-a-kind creations. This first example of an unknown maker's creel just has to be custom designed. The anchor, the fish and the sailboat all add aesthetic interest to this creel. All of the hobbies of the owner seem to have been inscribed for his or her pleasure. The geographical area that spawned this creel is unknown, but one would suspect that is from a coastal area, probably the Pacific Northwest.

The "wingtip" creel is truly a most unusual fish basket. It is a marvel of stitchery and design. It must have been a very cold and long winter when this nice basket was designed and leathered, for the work is complex and must have been very time consuming. It is unfortunate that there are no other known works in this genre.

This creel is called the "wingtip" creel because of all the small holes in the leather pieces, both horizontally and vertically, that resemble old wingtip shoes.

Other unmarked leather creels are embossed with a leaf pattern that looks like a vine. The baskets are Asian made and the leather used is of a good quality cowhide. Some of the leaf creels are leathered with a very heavy leather. The leaf embossing wheel produces a very appealing design and these leaf creels make a fine addition to any collection.

Quite a few creels have turned up with the same leaf embossing pattern.

In themselves, early center-hole leathered creels are rare, but when three show up, all leathered by the same hand, it is a real find! These creels are believed to be early Oregon made and hand-stamped by someone who certainly knew what he was about. The strap is original and the fastener is unusual. These creels could date to the turn of the century.

Leather for creels came from many sources. One craftsman used a very good green stained, French weave basket to make a creel by using the remains of an old U.S. Cavalry saddle bag. The "U.S." is still faintly visible of the front leather piece near the buckle. Unique and singular, this creel would have a great story to tell, if only it could speak.

Several early center hole creels with this design and construction have turned up. This one is in excellent condition. The earlier the creel, the more difficult it is to trace.

The leather for this creel is from an old set of cavalry saddle bags as indicated by the "U.S." stamp just below the buckle on the front piece of the leather.

There is no limit to the amount of leather a maker might use on a creel. Here is one completely leathered, front and back. With the fly and leader pocket in the back, this creel is an old wonder. The glow of the patina makes this creel jump out at you. The owner displays it with several other creels, but this one overpowers the others. An all-leather beauty, it begs to be displayed on its own.

Shown here are the front and back of a creel almost completely covered with leather. The wicker only shows at the ends of the creel. Note the pocket on the back.

This older, very long creel was undoubtedly used by
a fisherman who went after large fish.

10

Wickerwork Creels

A s unknown as many of the leatherers of creels are, the makers of the plain wicker baskets are even more unknown. This is for the simple reason that there were many more basket makers throughout the country.

One of the names that has survived, however, is that of Nick Mousel, of Yakima, Washington, a basket maker without peer. Originally from Luxembourg, Mousel arrived in the Yakima Valley sometime after the first World War. He made all sorts of baskets, clothes hampers, picnic baskets, wood baskets for fireplaces and, of course, creels. The willow he used was gathered along the rivers and creeks in the valley. The fabulous strength of his creels came from his use of whole willow. There is even a legend that has an auto running over one of his creels with no damage to either the auto or the creel! The story comes with a fisherman's name and a place in Canada where the alleged incident took place.

Mousel boiled his willow, peeled the bark, and kept it wet for ease in weaving. He made three sizes: small, medium and large. The latch was made of spring wire and screw eyes. He did make special order creels in larger sizes, and at least one big enough to require two latches.

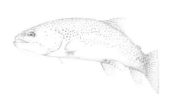

Nick Mousel used a unique double-wire latch on the handmade wicker creels he constructed in Yakima, Washington.

SHAKER WICKER STYLE

At one time there were eighteen Shaker communities from Kentucky and Ohio to New York and New England. They were driven by their devotion to labor and spirituality. The furniture that they designed and made, their baskets and oval containers, and the knit sweaters and clothing, all are distinctive in their simple design and masterful execution. All of the Shaker handicrafts have been copied by others, and their furniture is much replicated. This may also be true of some of the so-called "Shaker style" creels.

The Shakers made utilitarian objects: gathering baskets for the field, small baskets for personal use and baskets for the kitchen and storage. Most were plain, but a few were twined for decoration.

Many of the creels referred to as "Shaker" do have some characteristics of Shaker work, but not enough to identify them as such without reservation. We do know of one for sure. This creel, a camp creel or a salmon creel, came from the Sabbathday Lake community in Maine. The distinguishing characteristic is the copper wire reinforcement at the bottom of the creel. This basket was probably made for one of the community members who fished in the nearby waters. If a creel has all of the necessary attributes including the copper reinforcement at the bottom and a good provenance, it is definitely "Shaker." Similar creels are called "Shaker style" creels.

Originating in a Shaker community in Maine, this creel has two layers of wicker on the
bottom fastened together with copper wire.

This is the basic Cumings wicker creel with typical wooden latch. This creel came in many sizes and was sold through tackle dealers.

ED CUMINGS, INC.

"Ed Cumings, Inc., An Organization of Veteran Anglers, Flint, Michigan" was an organization of wholesalers of tackle and equipment sold by the "leading jobbers from coast to coast." The Ed Cumings catalog explains that the creels were made in Michigan of Michigan willow, "shaped to fit the body, and finished with spar varnish to prevent rotting."

In 1938 Cumings had five different creels available in several sizes. The "Midget" for children and the "Broadhead" were in the "Lifetime" line, as were the "High-Boy" and the "Bass-Boy." The "Standard" seems to be of similar quality but was not listed as a "Lifetime." The "Broadhead" was a lowboy-style available in 12- and 15-inch models. The "Standard" came in 12-, 14-, and 17- inch lengths, while the "Bass-Boy" was an 18-incher. The Cumings products were found in the great retail sporting goods houses such as Abercrombie & Fitch and Chicago's VL&A. A special metal tag was attached to the back of the creels that spelled out the VL&A address at "9 North Wabash, Chicago, Ill."

An unusual, tall, well-made wicker creel, this one was probably made by someone associated with Cumings using their construction methods.

WICKER CREELS

There were thousands of basket makers over the years in this country. Almost every town of any size had a basket maker to provide for the needs of the community. Many of these basket makers tried their hand at making creels from time to time as the need arose. There were many of these creel makers in the commercial trade, but few of their weavings have survived with the name attached.

The word "wicker" refers to a method of weaving baskets. In a wicker basket, the warp or vertical element is inflexible while the weft or horizontal element is flexible and is worked around the warp. Many different materials are used in making a wicker basket. The most common materials are rattan and willow.

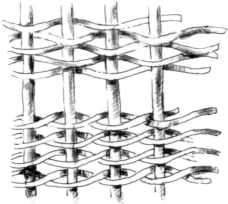

Wickerwork

This creel from Maine is made out of thin twigs woven between thin metal wire posts that connect the top and bottom.

Another creel originating in Maine, this one has a 1950s overshoes latch and a nicely finished center hole.

Made in the 1930s by a
Cherokee, this basket was
stained with berry juice to
produce an impressive
wicker creel.

A rounded bottom and scalloped lid make this wicker
creel a nice hanging decorator piece.

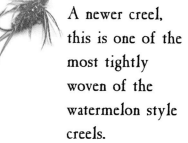

A newer creel,
this is one of the
most tightly
woven of the
watermelon style
creels.

This sturdy creel was built to sit on the ground and was possibly even used as a stool. It has a narrow hole for small fish and a solid metal latch.

This very thin but long creel was probably designed to minimize the creel's interference with the angler's arms while fishing.

Rattan, from the jungles of the Far East, is one of the most popular materials because it is light, strong and flexible. Round, long vines are gathered and stripped of leaves; the vines are then graded and tied into bundles by size. The smallest diameter, "size one", is considered the most valuable. Easy to identify, rattan is consistent in size and "hairy" in appearance. Willow, on the other hand, is not always the same size, has a smooth surface, and is not always consistent in flexibility. Sometimes it cracks as it is wickered. The split willow is much more flexible and can be twisted as it is woven.

This creel reminds one of a clothes hamper. It seems to have been commercially manufactured and different sizes have been found.

This basket maker used a
dark strand between two
lighter strands to produce a
beautifully woven creel.

This is a fairly common creel; it is featured in mid-20th century Orvis advertising.

Other materials such as roots or vines, particularly grape vines, have been used to make wicker creels. Variation can also be accomplished by splitting the elements into flat strands. As each basket maker strove to weave a better creel, all sorts of shapes and styles emerged. Because this was a commercial operation, visual appeal was important as well, and various coloring techniques were tried. Consequently, many interesting and appealing forms of wicker creels were produced.

European Creels

The English provide us with the earliest of the creels. In the later part of the 19th century, the major tackle distributors started showing creels in their catalogs. This created a need for larger quantities of consistent quality.

The early English creels were clearly one-of-a-kind handmade products. The Hardy's Perfect for example, hinged on the outside. These front hinged basket lids made it easier to access the interior without unslinging the basket. Others had side holes and separate compartments on the inside to carry fly wallets or bait containers, or even another small basket designed to hold live mayflies. There were some unusual variations, such as the netting Hardy added to the front to carry some extra clothing, a lunch bag, or even a very large fish. Some were made with a canvas cover to protect the wicker or willow. The canvas had a few pockets sewn to it. Other variants are seen in the very large backpack style panniers that the ghillies of the United Kingdom carried.

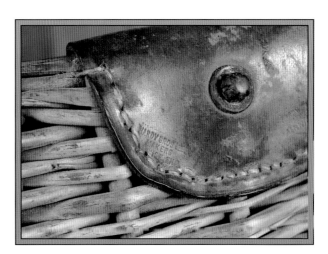

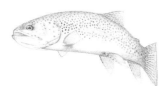

The Hardy "Perfect." This creel features netting on the front to carry equipment. Note the lid opens from back to front and there is a hole on the left side for the fish.

HARDY

To quote their famous catalog, the "Hardy's Angler's Guide" in 1872, Hardy Brothers Limited "commenced business as ... Fishing Rod and Tackle Makers ... (W)e have given to the angler not only the benefit of our experience as expert manufacturers, but the knowledge gained by a family of accomplished anglers." By the end of the 1930s, Hardys had, by Royal Warrant of Appointment, been named suppliers to such great anglers as His Majesty King George V, His Royal Highness the Prince of Wales, His Majesty the King of Spain, His Majesty the King of Italy, and most of the other royals of Europe along with many of the gentlemen anglers of the United States and Canada. Hardy Brothers of Alnwick were the suppliers. It is fitting then, that we begin with a showing of their fine products. Using both English and French willow, Hardy provided both wickered and French weave creels.

Probably the best known of the Hardy Brother creels is the handsome "Perfect." With a net for added carrying space, this could have been their most popular single creel. We see more of this model in fine condition than any other of their early offerings. Hinged on the outside, this made it much easier for the angler to access the interior of the basket.

The "Carry All" was just what the name implied. It was a tool used by the angler to carry all of his or her needs while on the stream. It had two compartments, one for the fish and over it another for the sundries all fishermen need to carry. The early "Carry Alls" had brass fittings. The latch carried the Hardy mark. This creel was made of whole English willow.

The two-decker creel on these two pages is the Hardy "Carry All." The top deck is for supplies and the hole goes through to the bottom for the fish. The big brass strap is marked with the patent date.

The Hardy "Houghton" comes in different sizes and with the hole in different places.

The whole willow creel with the extra straps was called the "Houghton." Woven with extra heavy willow at the bottom, this was the heavy duty model, made to take a little extra abuse. It came in several sizes for different types of angling.

This is a smaller Hardy "Houghton." The straps on the lid are used to hold a jacket or other equipment.

This early Farlow
French weave creel
came with or
without leather and/
or a brass buckle.

FARLOW

According to their 74th annual catalog, C. Farlow & Co. Ltd. was established in 1840 in London by Charles Farlow. That same catalog provides us with a description of "Stained Wicker Baskets, leather bound with brass mounts." In twenty years this creel had hardly changed. Still, possessing the best quality French weave—as well as being stained and varnished—these creels are particularly notable for their leather hinges. The sizes offered are numbered, and these numbers and sizes compare to those offered by Lawrence.

This is a very small Farlow-style creel. When the fish were small, why carry a big creel?

It appears that
people were
concerned about
lively fish jumping
out of their creels,
so Farlow put a
flap over the hole
on this one.

In a later refinement, several sizes of the stained basket had leather findings and binding on the edges of the top. These center hole French weave baskets were very attractive in appearance. Sometimes leather straps were added to the top to carry one's coat. These creels would be a grand addition to any collection.

Leather corners were an even further refinement, and a leather flap was added for the hole. The top straps were already there, and it is interesting to further note that this was the first English-made creel that carried corner leather reinforcing.

This is a later Farlow, but it still has many of the early features. The straps on the lid are for a jacket and other gear.

"Wicker with tray" was offered in the 'teens, but by 1935 had disappeared from the catalog. It compares with the Hardy "Carry All" but there are differences. The Farlow has leather bound edges and corners.

Named for the famous river, the "Test" did not have a hole in the top, but rather had the top hinged in the middle to open fore and aft rather than in the accepted manner. This design was not copied by many latter day creel makers, apparently because it was not very functional.

This is another version of the "Carry All." Other companies sold them besides Hardy.

This is the English "Test" style creel. Instead of a hole, there was a hinge in the middle of the lid and one opened half the creel for fish or equipment.

McPhearson of Scotland was one of the earliest makers to sew leather over large portions of wicker creels. This example shows almost half a French weave creel covered with leather.

MCPHEARSON

McPhearson, Scotland's popular supplier of fishing tackle, was known to have leathered classic creels as early as 1884. The full leathered top and the extra wide center stripe make this a most attractive collectable. The "frugal" Scottish needed to prolong the useful life of their equipment, so the addition of leather was not just logical, it was sensible. McPhearson's handwork and practical eye for design make these creels extremely collectable.

Even the English with their sense of history have unknown creel makers. The very old creel shown with the full leathered top is very much like the McPhearson, but was done by a different hand.

There is no mark on this early leathered creel. It appears to be English.

The history of English creels also includes other less famous makers such as "Little of Haymarket, London" and "Foster Brothers of Ashbourn." From the time of Isaak Walton to the present, the English have had a profound influence on the art of the fishing creel.

Many English style creels are also not marked.

For many years, this old English creel hung on the wall of the "Creel Lodge" in Turangi, New Zealand.

Here is a later model double-decker creel with no maker's mark on it.

This large bag with an old net is typical of what a ghilly might carry to hold his client's fish.

This combination of wicker basket and canvas bag is called a "Conway." This one was made by Brody Halesowen and is about twenty years old.

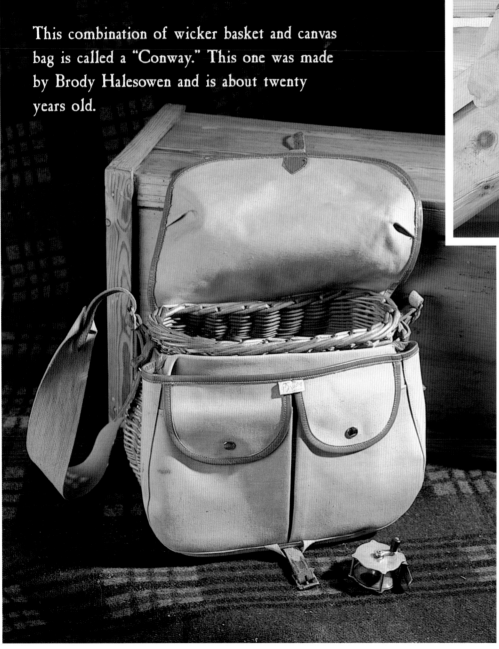

At the end of the day, the keeper would hang his coat and bag and retire for a pipe and a dram. The net makes this interesting musette bag a very collectable item.

Brody Halesowen, another well-known tackle purveyor, featured an overcoat for a wicker willow creel. Because of the condition of the examples we have seen, it appears that this creel, called the "Conway," came late, after 1920.

These two fishing bags are classic examples of leather English bags.

Well-formed pannier with metal legs.

At last we have a picture of the old pannier. It certainly hasn't changed much since Isaak Walton's day. The ghillies used them to carry everything, including the large salmon caught by the party. These baskets were strong enough to sit on, and the sportsman need only carry the Hardy bag shown here as a convenient place to keep his tackle.

In use since the 1700s, this large wicker basket is called a pannier.
Built with legs, they have the strength to be used as stools. Contrast
this to the simple Hardy bag for the fisherman on the move.

OTHER EUROPEAN CREELS

Other European countries besides the U.K., such as France, Portugal, and Germany also produce creels. American tackle retailer Abercrombie & Fitch proudly touts creels from Austria and Italy, and the Belgians contribute a classic whole willow creel with a distinctive wooden latch. Some French creels purchased in France by American anglers show pegs at the back of the creel that acted as levelers for when the basket was placed on the ground. The best of the French creels are those that the English called "French weave." They were split willow, twined in the weaving in an attractive manner, and were copied by almost all the creel making world. While most of the woven baskets were simple in design, these creels took very deft and practiced fingers to complete the complex demands of the French weave.

Besides the French weave, some French creels also feature pegs on the back corners to allow the creel to sit on flat surfaces.

This common whole willow creel was made in Belgium. Belgian creels are frequently stamped on the bottom.

An Abercrombie & Fitch product, this creel was manufactured for them in Italy.

Asian Creels

Asia has produced a huge number of creels, particularly since World War II. Most of the creels leathered in the U.S. came from Asia originally. After the war, Asia began to produce their own leathered creels and exported them to the U.S. Since then, the American production of leathered creels has pretty well dried up.

Some pockets are fairly standard and many of this Asian-style creel have been produced.

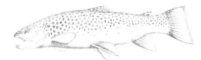

The standard Asian baskets come in both French weave and whole wicker style. They also come with a variety of latches. Note the two fish designs.

This creel was made in Occupied Japan. It has a pocket made of thin leather which has curled over time.

Shipped in large containers, the baskets arrived in this country complete except for carrying straps. The creels had self-hinges, a straw loop hanger at the back of the basket and a leather and metal latching gadget of some sort. Even some of these latches can be collectible, especially those that were fish-shaped. Several things happened after arrival. If the importer was a leatherer—Lawrence for example—he would decide how many to leather, remove the latches, loops, and hinges and the stripped baskets would be sent to the leathering people to complete. The rest of the shipment would be offered for sale as plain creels. The two fine examples that we have show how the baskets looked on arrival.

The Japanese began making and exporting creels around the turn of the century. They specialized in French weave creels. The earliest had center holes and very tight weaves. In the 1910s they switched to offset holes for right-handed casters. Over the years, the weave got looser and the split willow strands got wider. Also, there is a school of thought that dates Japanese creels according to the width of the wrapped whole willow stems on the bottom of the creel. The earlier creels have a narrower wrapped base that the French weave is attached to.

The double pockets on the front of a Japanese creel are unusual. Again, the thin leather is beginning to curl.

The leather covers half of the lid and makes this a very nice, rare Japanese creel.

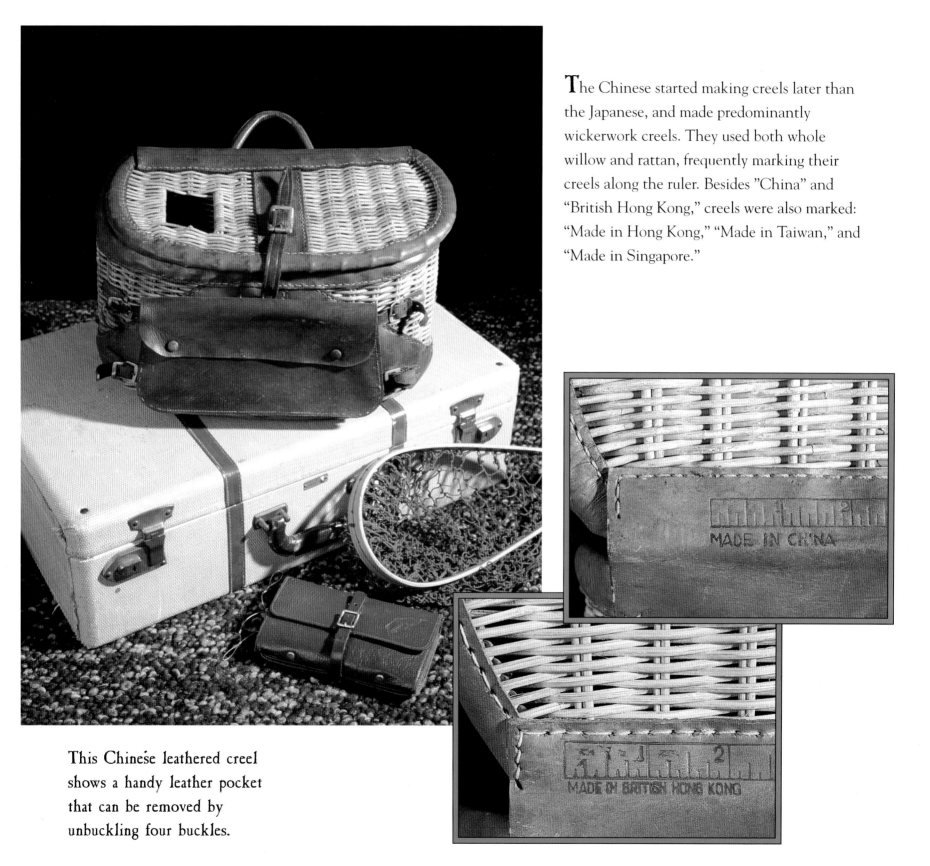

The Chinese started making creels later than the Japanese, and made predominantly wickerwork creels. They used both whole willow and rattan, frequently marking their creels along the ruler. Besides "China" and "British Hong Kong," creels were also marked: "Made in Hong Kong," "Made in Taiwan," and "Made in Singapore."

MADE IN CHINA

MADE IN BRITISH HONG KONG

This Chinese leathered creel shows a handy leather pocket that can be removed by unbuckling four buckles.

The Chinese also put leather
pockets on the front of
their creels.

This creel is quite unusual, as it has the hole on the other side of the lid for left-handers.

Asian creels were leathered with two simple designs. They range in size from a salesman's sample to large enough to hold a steelhead. Note the "arrow pattern" on the large creel.

One of the prime importers of Asian-made creels was the Los Angeles Saddle and Findings Co, LASFCO. The company was a wholesaler and manufacturer representative of many products for the leather trade including creels. The creels that it imported were mainly the plain split willow French weave that others used to leather, but without a doubt, they brought in leathered examples that are not hard to identify.

The manufacturers of most of the Asian creels used a simple arrow pattern. The typical leather runs from near the top center front of the basket obliquely down to the corners. Sometimes the top edges were trimmed and some of the late imports came with fly pockets buckled or sewn to the front. These are also noted for their back handles that are made of grass enclosed in leather. There is a stitch pattern in the middle of the back leather reinforcement that is distinctive. One of the customs of Asian culture is for craftsmen to produce great pieces of work without marking them with their name. There are undoubtedly many of these "unknown craftsmen" who made creels, but there is very little chance of identifying the maker now.

Sometimes a creel is special because of the owner. In this case, the creel belonged to Omar Needham, a cane rod maker who worked for Orvis.

It is probable that this flood of leathered creels arriving from cheap labor markets in Asia spelled the end to the American leathered creel.

If not removed by the importer, one can sometimes find on a pristine creel, a paper label that names the country of origin. The "Made in Occupied Japan" dates and places the creel. One more indicator of country of origin may be found on the ruler. But the collector should know that many of these markings have been removed by scraping. With this in mind, any scratches on the rulers ought to be carefully examined.

Someone painted flowers on this creel's leather; a flower child from California, or a folk artist from Appalachia.

This checkerwork creel is a very unusual creel. Note the center hole.

Metal Creels

Creels are sometimes made from materials other than wicker and leather. Surprisingly, some makers have used metal to make their creels or to add to the wicker. The tops of some very nice wickerwork creels, both plain and leathered, were replaced by a metal lid that did many jobs: bait can, stretcher for snelled flies or lead weight container. These were just a few of the options available. On some creels, there was even a tray for a sandwich. There were several makers of these tops, including L. Quinn and Co., Milwaukee, Wisconsin and Handitop of Los Angeles, California and Portland, Oregon.

When opened up, the Quinn top shows compartments for hooks, sinkers, etc., and a hooking device to carry snelled hooks.

In order to solve the problem of what to do with fishing "stuff," some creel makers began using metal tops on creels. The hole in the top goes through to the bottom for the fish.

Here, a leathered creel has had the lid replaced with a Handitop. Recognize the embossing? This creel is a Lawrence "Supreme."

The December 31, 1922 issue of the *Oregon Magazine* announced a new invention:

> *"A new tackle carrier is the Handitop Fish Basket, invented by Mr. R.E. Eaton of LaPine, Oregon … Mr. Eaton, as other fishermen do, experienced much difficulty in keeping his fish tackle together, and very frequently while on fishing trips, he would lose or leave at home something that he wanted to use … Mr. Eaton has taken Mr. D. V. Glenn as a partner, forming the company of Eaton & Glenn, and the Company is now manufacturing the Handitop in Portland, Oregon."*

The Handitop had a bait can that rotated to allow access for the fish. The entire top then lifted to allow access to the basket. Lawrence creels, both marked and not, have been found with Handitops and Quinn tops.

When you open a Handitop, you find space for snelled hooks, etc., and a bait canteen in the middle.

This woven aluminum creel was made after World War II.

Another metal group that adds to the presence and value of the folk art creel is the checkerworked aluminum creels made after World War II. These creels were made of aircraft aluminum splints. The craftsmanship is excellent and the design is attractive. While they probably were not a commercial success, these aluminum creels deserve a place in a broad based creel collection. They make a statement like that of a piece of metal sculpture.

 Here is a different kind of aluminum woven creel. It is very sturdy with strong loops to fasten the shoulder harness.

The most unusual feature of this creel is the design on the front and sides. Each indentation was stamped out from the inside by hand.

Using metal as a medium, craftsmen have endeavored to construct the most functional and appealing creels.

Like the basket makers and the leathersmiths, the metal workers got creative in their attempts to produce a better creel. They punched holes of various kinds for ventilation and tried different shapes and sizes. Someone even constructed a metal frame and wove marine cordage on the frame to produce a remarkable creel.

A metal frame provides the structure for this creel. Twisted twine was then woven onto the frame to make this a metal and string creel.

Utilitarian is the best word to describe this all-metal creel. With holes for drainage and a single hole for fish in the lid, the maker certainly knew something about fishing.

Contemporary Creels

There are still makers and leatherers of creels. In Seattle, Washington, and in various places in Oregon, there are weavers of baskets and individuals and firms who can and will add wonderful leatherwork to their handwoven product. Daryll Whitehead, one of the earliest and most important collectors of old fishing creels, is also a basket maker. Whitehead, now retired from service in the federal government, is a maker of cane fly rods, and a metalworker who makes reel seats and line guides. In 1993, Whitehead took a basket making class from Debbie McClelland of Seattle. As he became more proficient, his style developed. He now weaves his creels over a beautiful wooden form provided by an old pattern maker. When baskets are completed, he generally sends them to Freeman Mariner to be leathered.

A contemporary basket made by Daryll Whitehead using black stained strips to produce a stunning arrow design.

One of his first efforts, this Mariner
creel exhibits his fine craftsmanship.

Mariner, a retired Customs Agent (who walked across Europe with George Patton's Third Army) does impressive decorative leather work. His carving and stamping are a step beyond. His leaping fish are superb!

Mariner's first leather work was in designing and making holsters in an attempt to find a comfortable way to carry a pistol. He then graduated to repairing reel boxes and gun leather for Whitehead. Later he made leather rod cases and reel boxes. His real challenge came when he had to repair a creel and antique the new leather to match the old. He carved his first fish on a reel box, and in 1993, Mariner concluded his training period, going on to leathering new creels created by Whitehead.

Daryll Whitehead, seated with his basket form, and Freeman Mariner, are two of the fine creel craftsmen working today.

A creel collector
commissioned
jumping fish on his
Mariner creel.

Mariner's leathered creels are masterpieces of folk art. Some have called him "The Myth" because after one East Coast auction sale (of a Mariner leathered creel), Whitehead was told that Mariner was a myth, that Whitehead himself had leathered the basket. Well, no denials were to be believed.

A fine Mariner creel, basket stamped, and with
a beautifully designed harness and shoulder strap.

Jumping fish on the lid make this Freeman Mariner creel
one of the most spectacular creels ever made.

These very appealing center hole creels were
masterfully leathered by Freeman Mariner.

Arne Mason of Ashland, Oregon—another contemporary leather craftsman—makes superb reproductions of the old English leather potbellied creels. He has done some excellent research to make his product authentic. The Leather Conservation Centre in Northhampton, England, provided Arne with much of the facts necessary to produce his creels. In one of his interesting asides, Arne pointed out that there was a lot of pressure on the fisheries in England during the 18th Century because of the need-for cheap protein. That pressure reduced the size of the fish, explaining the small hole in the top of this fine 18th century replica.

Arne Mason carefully researched old English creels to make this authentic reproduction of an 18th century creel.

David G. Nay carved a top for an old Asian leathered creel, stamped his cartouche on it, and sewed the new leather onto the existing top. His rendering of a jumping fish taking a fly is excellent.

A contemporary artist, David G. Nay releathered the top of this creel using a fish motif.

There are other contemporary basket makers at work in the creel business today, which is good news. It is great to know that the art of the creel is still being carried on by dedicated craftsmen.

This older center hole creel was releathered to add artistic appeal. It appears in a logo for a store as a symbol of angling.

Authors' Acknowledgments

The real heroes of this book are the creel collectors. They invited us into their homes to photograph their creels and put up with hours of disruption, mess, and discussion about their collection. A few collectors even risked their beloved creels to UPS or the U.S. Postal Service in order to help this book as much as they could. Beyond their creels and their hospitality, their faith in this book contributed the energy and the enthusiasm to keep this project going. We are deeply grateful to:

Roger Baker
Gary Carbaugh
Dan and Gail Cook
Gary Estabrook
Rich Gardiner
Bob and Arlene Hanson
Ernie Johnson
Ralph and Martha Lapham
Brian McGrath
Bruce and Amy Miller
Terry Ow
Gordon Patton
Carl and Jeannette Pergam
Dean Shank
John Stuart
Daryll Whitehead
Tom and Lesly Williams

As the book unfolded we needed information and technical assistance, and it seemed that someone was there with enthusiastic help and valuable information whenever we needed it. We appreciate the technical assistance provided by:

Dan Abrams
Rebecca Andrews
Craig Bates
Georg Beimel
Steve Eich
Pam Endzweig
Herb Hornstra
Martha Labell
Bill Lawrence III
Mary Jane Lenz
Marsha Mathews
John Putnam
Gerald Rosenthal
Sieglinde Smith
Laila Williamson

The team that produced this book worked long and hard to bring this book to life. The hardest worker was Gretchen Duykers who waded streams, climbed fences, rode airplanes and cheerfully put up with inane questions in her zeal to photograph each creel perfectly. David Allen and Leroy Redonovich photographed the creels that Gretchen couldn't get to. Taking photographs was just the beginning of the work. We thank the following people for ably providing the production skills necessary to get the book to press:

Jeff Burgard
Bruce Duykers
Jan French
Marcia Rueter Leritz
Martha Lonner
Mary Myers
John and Bobbie McClain
Lynn Rosenthal
Lang Smith
Ed Totten

There is no question that the most important source of enthusiasm for this project came from Jeanne and Mary. For their support of our crazy creel addiction, we thank them and love them very much.

What started out as an opportunity to purchase a creel collection has turned into a remarkable adventure. We have been privileged to hold and photograph many amazing works of art, and we have come to feel responsible for doing justice to this wonderful art form. The people we met have inspired and supported us in our challenge to bring *The Art of the Creel* to life. We are very thankful that the opportunity to do this project came to us.

Hugh Chatham
Dan McClain

References

Abercrombie & Fitch Co.; *The Appeal of Angling* 1934

At the British Engineerium; *One Man One Rod* 1932

Bowman, John S.; *Shaker Style* 1995

Calabi Silvio; *The Collector's Guide to Antique Fishing Tackle* 1989

Farlow's 93rd Edition 1933

Farlow C. & Co., Limited; *Fishing Tackle Manufacturing* 1908

Graham, Jamie Maxtone; *The Best of Hardy's Anglers' Guide* 1982

Graham, Jamie Maxton; *Fishing Tackle of Yesterday*

Hardy's Anglers' Guide 1930

Hardy's Anglers' Guide 1952

Hardy the House of; *Anglers' Guide and Catalog* 1934

Horrocks-Ibbotson Co.; *46th Edition* 1956

Irwin, John Rice; *Baskets an Basketmakers in Southern Appalachia* 1982

Jardine, Charles; *The Classic Guide to Fly Fishing For Trout* 1991

Keanne, Martin J.; *Classic Rods & Tackle* 1986

Keanne, Martin J.; *Classic Rods & Tackle* 1991

Kewley, Charles & Farrar, Howard; *Fishing Tackle For Collectors* 1987

Kylloe, Ralph; *Rustic Traditions* 1993

Lang, Bob; *Lang's Sporting Advertising & Sportsman's Auction* 1996

Lawson, George S. Jr.; *Lawson's Price Guide to Old Fishing Rods & Miscellaneous Tackle* 1997

Lawrence, George; *Catalogs* 1924, 1929, 1932, 1940, 1941, 1944, 1945, & 1952

Lobb, Allan; *Indian Baskets* 1989

Mason, Otis Tufton; *Aboriginal Indian Basketry* 1904

Miles, Charles; *Indian and Eskimo Artifacts of North America* 1963

Montgomery Ward; *Fishing and Hunting Catalog* 1950

Oliver, Richard; *High Rollers Public Auction of Fine Fishing Tackle & Accessories* 1991

Schlick, Mary Dodds; *Columbia River Basketry* 1994

Smith, Albert & Co. LTD; *Dominion Works, Redditch* 1926

Stewart, Hilary; *Indian Fishing Early Methods on the Northwest Coast* 1977

The Classic Chronicle - Summer 1996

Turner, Graham; *Fishing Tackle - A Collector's Guide* 1989

VL&A; *Best of Sport Catalog* 1951

VomHofe, Edward & Co.; *Fine Fishing Tackle* 1933

White, Philip; *Trout Fly Fishing* 1994

Wright, Robert K.; *A Time of Gathering* 1991

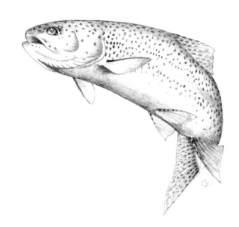

Index